Habitats

DOUGLAS FIR

WENDY DAVIS

⊄Ρ Children's Press

A Division of Grolier Publishing
New York London Hong Kong Sydney
Danbury, Connecticut

Created and Developed by The Learning Source

Designed by Josh Simons

Acknowledgments: We wish to thank the people and organizations, especially Tom Stack, who provided technical assistance with this project. Their help is greatly appreciated.

All illustrations by Glenn Quist

Photo Credits: Gerry Ellis/Ellis Nature Photography: 14-15, 20 (background), 21, 25 (top), 26, 28, 29, 32, backcover; The Learning Source: 8; Tom & Pat Leeson: cover, 1, 3-7, 10-13, 16-19, 20 (inset), 22 (right), 23-24, 25 (bottom), 27; Tom Stack & Associates: 22 (left, center).

Library of Congress Cataloging-in-Publication Data
Davis, Wendy.
      Douglas fir / by Wendy Davis.
             p. cm. — (Habitats)
      Summary: Describes the growth of a Douglas fir sapling in an old growth forest in the northwestern United States and the other plants and animals that are part of its habitat.
      ISBN 0-516-20712-1 (lib. bdg.) ISBN 0-516-26064-2 (pbk.)
         1. Douglas fir—Northwest, Pacific—Juvenile literature.
2. Douglas fir—Ecology-Northwest, Pacific—Juvenile literature.
3. Forest ecology—Northwest, Pacific—Juvenile literature.
4. Forest animals—Northwest, Pacific—Juvenile literature.
[1. Douglas fir. 2. Trees. 3. Forest ecology. 4. Ecology.]
I. Title. II. Series: Habitats (Children's Press)
QK494.5.P66D38 1997
585'.2—dc21

                        96-51027
                        CIP
                        AC

Printed in the United States of America

4 5 6 7 8 9 10 R 06

In the northwestern part of the United States, forests often grow so thick that sunlight barely reaches the ground. Here, the trees can live for nearly 1,000 years. These places are called Old Growth forests.

Fallen logs lie all along the forest floor, rotting for centuries. And like a thick carpet, velvety moss covers everything in sight. In the deep, crowded forest, time seems to stretch out forever.

Life is everywhere in these forests. Herds of elk come to nibble on young trees.

Hungry raccoons search for fish in icy streams. Black bears climb on sturdy tree trunks, looking for something good to eat.

Deep in one such forest, a baby Douglas fir tree grows. The sapling, as young trees are called, has taken root on an old, dead log. This is a nurse log, and it is a fine place for a sapling to grow.

Without sunlight, the little tree would die. So its branches and needles struggle upward toward the sun.

A nurse log feeds and protects the sapling until it is ready to live on its own. The nurse log takes in water. Then it holds the water, like a huge sponge, for the sapling to drink.

Inside the log, insects, chemicals, bacteria, and other decomposers chew away at the wood. This rotting wood gives the sapling the food, or nutrients, it needs to grow.

Down below, the roots of the sapling work hard, too. They stretch out through and around the nurse log, looking for food and water in the soil. And meanwhile, under the ground, truffles—a kind of mushroom—grow on the roots of the young tree.

Truffles are important to the tree. They give the tree added food and water. In turn, the tree gives the truffles sugar, which they need in order to live. Without truffles, a young tree would not live very long.

For some forest dwellers, like tree voles or flying squirrels, truffles are a tasty treat. The animals dig for them using their sharp claws.

The mouselike tree vole is about 5 inches long. It usually is gray in color, with short legs and tiny ears. Along with flying squirrels, tree voles help spread truffles around the forest to the trees that need them.

As the animals dig, sharp eyes carefully watch every movement. This spotted owl is just waiting for the chance to dine on a vole or a flying squirrel tonight.

The sapling grows and grows. In time, the nurse log decomposes, or falls apart. Now the young tree is able to live on its own.

Without the nurse log, the base of the tree can look odd, as if it is standing on tiptoe.

Finally, after many years, the full-grown Douglas fir stands 200 or perhaps even 300 feet (61 to 90 meters) tall. Like its neighbors, it is full of old woodpecker holes and is home to many living things.

Most important, the tree is now part of the forest canopy. It will most likely live for a very long time.

The canopy, or roof of the forest, is where the tops of tall trees meet. Moss and other plants grow thick there, fed by the light of the sun.

The canopy is a giant garden in which insects, birds, and animals live and eat. It also shades the forest floor and protects creatures from the weather.

Birds such as this evening grosbeak usually build their nests high in the canopy. They feed on the many insects that hide up here in the moss.

Eagles nest in the canopy, too. Perched so high,
they are able to spot their prey from a long way off.

At the base of the Douglas fir, animals busy themselves. Spotted grouse and shy deer hide their young in bushes. They hope to keep the babies safe from the quick-moving weasels and fishers that come to hunt.

Fishers, with their brown and grayish fur, live in holes high up in the trees. When fishers hunt they use their great leaping ability to chase squirrels and other animals through the treetops and onto the ground.

During its lifetime, strong winds and heavy snow cause the tree to lose some branches. The hollow left by a broken branch creates a safe nesting spot for this family of tiny hummingbirds.

The Douglas fir lives for a very long time. But as with all living things, old age causes it to weaken. In time, the old tree dies, killed by insects, disease, and storms.

But death is not the end for the Douglas fir. In thick Old Growth forests, a dead tree often continues to stand for 200 years or even longer. A dead tree that remains standing is called a snag.

The snag now becomes home to new kinds of creatures. Ladybugs, beetles, and other insects rush in and eat away at the tree from the inside out.

Newts come, too, darting in and out of the snag's rotted parts. Even bears find cozy little homes in the snag's hollow base. A snag house might be just the place to spend the long, cold winter.

Finally, the snag grows too weak to stand and falls to the ground. Now even more plants and animals move into the fallen log. Raccoons find homes in old woodpecker holes, once too high to reach.

Mushrooms grow in and around the log. Slugs and insects move in, too. Together, they break down the rotting wood into soil. In 500 years or so, the log will be completely gone.

But in the meantime, seed cones are falling from nearby trees. Sometimes, winds or birds or animals knock them down. Sometimes, it is simply time for them to fall.

Trees like the Douglas fir have two kinds of cones, male and female. In the spring, wind carries pollen dust from the male cones to the female ones. As the female cone ripens, the seeds of new Douglas fir trees are formed.

All around the fallen log, squirrels and mice nibble at the cones. Tiny seeds catch onto their bodies . . . or are eaten and passed out in their droppings.

In time, some of the seeds come to rest on the old log. A few of them take root. Now the once-great Douglas fir becomes a nurse log itself.

Soon, a new sapling rises up through the darkness of the forest, struggling to reach the sunlight. Maybe, just maybe, it will grow tall and strong. Then it, too, might live for a thousand years or more as part of the Old Growth forest.

More About

Roosevelt Elk, Page 6:
Only male elk have antlers. Antlers grow during the summer and are shed late in winter. Some measure up to 5 feet (1.5 meters) from tip to tip.

Flying Squirrel, Page 10:
Flying squirrels cannot actually fly. Instead, they glide from tree to tree, using loose skin on their legs like a kind of parachute.

Raccoon, Page 7:
Raccoons can handle objects almost as skillfully as monkeys. Raccoons often use their paws to dunk food into water before eating it.

Spotted Owl, Page 11:
Spotted owls are not only wise and curious. They're talkative, too. They can hoot at other owls in at least 13 different ways.

Black Bear, Page 7:
A black bear will tear apart a beehive to get at the honey it loves to eat. The bear's thick fur protects it from being stung almost everywhere, except on the nose.

Douglas fir, Page 14:
A fully grown Douglas fir may have 60 million needles. Like leaves, the needles turn sunlight into food and keep the tree alive and healthy.

This Habitat

Eagle, Page 17:
Eagles build huge nests called aeries (AIR eez) and add to them year after year. An old aerie may measure 10 feet (3 meters) across and 20 feet (6 meters) deep.

Hummingbird, Page 20:
Hummingbirds do not really hum. This name comes from the sound their wings make as they beat up to 70 times per second.

Spotted Grouse, Page 18:
When it is time to find a mate, male grouse first fight one another. Then the winners do a kind of dance to attract the females.

Newt, Page 22:
Newts are a type of salamander. They begin life in water but spend several years on land. Like all amphibians, newts must return to the water to breed.

Weasel, Page 18:
When weasels are frightened they give off a bad-smelling liquid called musk. (Skunks give off the same kind of liquid.) The smell can last for days on whatever has been sprayed.

Slug, Page 25:
A slug is a type of snail that has no shell. As it crawls a slug gives off a path of slime that protects it from sharp objects.